Color It Red

The Power of the Blood

Doris Hope

Unless otherwise noted, all Scripture quotations are from the King James Version of the Bible.

Color It Red
The Power of the Blood
ISBN-13: 978-0692099612

Copyright ©2018 by Doris Hope

Published by
H.O.P.E. Publishing

This book is available at special quantity discounts for bulk purchase for sales promotions, fund-raising and educational needs. For information please write authordorishope@gmail.com.

DEDICATION

This book is dedicated to you. Whosoever dares to pick up this book and accept the challenge to color "it" red, this book is for you. If you think that it's time to delete those negative dark spots and blemishes of yesterday from your life, then this book is for you. It's time to apply the Blood of Jesus for all those areas that resulted in more harm than good leaving your life stuck and stagnant without progress.

This book is dedicated to every female that is connected to me in some way. In special honor of those women that played an important role in my life. To my Queen Bee, my loving mother, Annie E. Hope; My Godmother, Sarah L. Moore: a special aunt, Margaret Ayres; my mentor, Pastor Cookie Williams, and my Pastor, Dr. Tamara T. Scott, all whom is such an inspiration in my life.

I dedicate this book to my daughter, granddaughters, goddaughters, god sisters, stepdaughters, daughters in love, sisters, nieces, cousins, mentees, friends and even my enemies, haters, doubters, and all of you "Peninnah's" in my life that provoked me, I'm coloring "it" red. I'm letting the past pass and I'm moving on and encouraging you to do the same.

ACKNOWLEDGMENTS

To my #1 Cheerleader, GOD, my Rock, Fortress, Strong Tower, Roots, Foundation, Strength and Life Line. He continuously bids me to come unto Him, where I am fortified for the journey. I Love You!

To my editor, Karen Rodgers, who faithfully pulls me through. Thank you for your contribution to my assignments. Critique Editing Services, LLC. www.critiqueyourbook.com. Krodgerseditor60@gmailcom

To Elder Wanza Leftwich for challenging the writing group to write, write, write. www.WanzaLeftwich.com.

Last, but not least, Keenya Kelly of If You Brand It that caught my vision and ran with it. Excellent cover. www.ifyoubrandit.com.

FOREWORD

I was introduced to Author Doris Hope's work in December of 2012 and was amazed at the depth of spiritual insight she displayed in her writing. I immediately found myself, and my issues, on the pages. With each topic she went deeper to explain what was going on inside me. How was that possible? I wondered. We've never met, how did she know me so well and yet not know me personally? I knew the answer, but I'd never experienced that level of ministry through a book before. It was as if she was being used by God to minister to me specifically. She was able to so closely pinpoint where I was in my walk and where I had gotten off track. But more incredible than that to me, she was able to pull my remedy off God's shelf—my Balm imported straight from Gilead—and she gently applied it to my wound and I was healed. I was completely blown away.

With *Color It Red* the exact same thing occurred. Bitterness had settled in my heart due to my inability to confront. I was always good for running away from a volatile situation, but the perpetrator always got off scot-free and I was left with a bag of pain, a scarred heart and electrical tape over my mouth. And my anger unexpressed turned to bitterness. I was a mess, but quite honestly, I had tamped my feelings so far down I didn't even know how severe my situation had become. Enter *Dr. Doris.* This book was introduced to me right on time and I devoured it, knowing God had sent the answer to my immediate issue and sure enough, surgery and healing ensued.

If you're in need of spiritual healing, this book will bless you. Author Doris Hope hears from God, of that I am convinced, and she can convey what she hears to her readers with scalpel sharp precision. God bless you as you read this book with an open mind and an open heart.

Karen H. Rodgers,
God's Grateful Girl

Table of Contents

INTRODUCTION

"WHAT? WHAT? "WHAT can wash away my sins? NOTHING but the blood of Jesus. What can make me whole again? Nothing but the blood of Jesus. Oh, precious is that flow, that makes me white as snow no other fount I know, nothing but the blood of Jesus." An old gospel hymn written by a Baptist minister name Robert Lowry in 1876. While our sin makes us unclean, broken, and disconnected from the Father, Jesus' blood will repair and restore us back to Him.

When a painter starts to paint a picture, sometimes he will have in mind the picture that he desires to be on the paper. He must strategically and intentionally sway that paintbrush back and forth, up and down, and even side to side until he begins to see on paper what he sees in his mind. Sometimes he must mix colors to get exactly what he desires or change the colors and even remove some colors to perfect that picture. Did you know that God is doing the same thing in each of our lives? He is bringing the good, bad, ugly, and uncomfortable events in each of our lives to full bloom, displaying all the negatives as well as the positives to let you know that He is in control. If your life feels like a picture with all different kinds of colors thrown on the paper and you cannot seem to make out the picture, this book is for you. I've been there so I know exactly how you feel.

Take a walk with me through the cemetery and let's imagine how many secrets, lies, deceptions, silent words, and broken hearts lie empowered by silence. Can you imagine with me how many "things" are still crying out at the place where there is now no life? How about how many answers are bedridden by death and the grave? Just think about how many untold truths now remain dormant because someone didn't want to hurt someone else's feelings, embarrass their family, or lose a so-called friend? We can go on and on creating scenarios that covers, prevents, and conceals an enemy of mass destruction, but the buck stops here. The war is over of years and years of inner struggles and silent frustrations. The truth must be exposed so that God's freedom can flow from the inside out.

Color It Red demonstrates the power of the blood of Jesus. Jesus died and shed his blood for our sins and it's because of his blood that we can live on, despite our past. Yes, the past has a way of trying to hold you captive in your heart and mind, but it's time to apply the blood and keep it moving. Jesus said in Matthew 26:28 (KJV) "For this is my blood of the new testament which is shed for many for the remission of sins." Let the blood do the work that it was sent to do.

Color It Red demonstrates how the things of yesterday can be forgiven and covered so that you can walk out your purpose and destiny. You do know that you have an enemy that is working full-time and overtime to block and stop you from fulfilling your purpose? He did not start today, but the day that you were born, to deplete you, and stagnate every gift, talent and ability that God invested in you to help someone else. We are encouraging you not to give your enemy the satisfaction that he thought he had while you walked around for years in silence, protecting everyone else except you. It's time to step up to the plate and uncover, expose, and decompose the forces of darkness that keeps you bound. Why be bound when you can be free? Romans 8:1 validates you by declaring, "Therefore, there is now no condemnation to them which are in Christ Jesus, who walk not after the flesh, but after the Spirit."

Color It Red demonstrates the power of the blood of Jesus. Those unspoken and hidden secrets and situations that make you think that your life is a mess is a message for others. No mess, no ministry; no trouble, no triumph; no wounds, no wisdom. God wants to use your life as a living testimony, despite your past, and your past doesn't have the power to hold you hostage, unless you allow it.

Take another walk with me but this time it is down the road of recovery as Jesus leads us towards our future. With the Blood of Jesus dripping behind us, as we continue to move forward, it is covering everything in the past, so that when our enemies try to check our past, the only thing that they will see, is the Blood of Jesus, because He colored it red.

CHAPTER ONE

Unveiling the Veil

Have you ever heard that saying, "What goes on in this house stays in this house?" Well I heard it being said so many times, but it did not hit home for me. My mother was a single parent, stayed to herself, and there was not a lot of activities going on at our house. Coincidentally, my aunt and her family lived next door so there was always company, but they were family, so when we had company, it was family.

Family is that wild, crazy and sometimes embarrassing two different groups of people that you can't disown because some of them resemble you. You can't write them off, because you need them, and they need you. You can't ignore them forever because everybody needs somebody. When all is said and done, family is always there, rather you are right or wrong. It's amazing how God put together these strangers that is called family and then you get to learn how to love them unconditionally, no matter what come and go.

The enemy do not like the structure of family and its purpose. He is not pleased with anything involving unity. Family brings the meaning of unity into focus. I believe it was designed with that purpose in mind because when I am united with my family, I could feel the love of unity. Even though we don't always agree, but it's ok to agree to disagree. We do not allow it to separate us though, but we continue to stay connected, no matter what.

I believe God incorporated family in the lives of his people so that no one must be alone. There is a void in each of us that is fulfilled when family comes together. One of my mottos is, "There's nothing like family!" Family time just bring pure joy, love, and strength to our relationships. While there may be bickering and arguing from some, it all ends in love. However, every family cannot describe their family reunions like I just described. As a matter of fact, it is totally the opposite. Their love for one another is shared in a totally different way. No, my family is no ways perfect, and we have our differences, but we were raised more like sisters and brothers than cousins, so we are close and looks out for one another.

Like a caring, thoughtful woman she was, my mother tried to protect her three girls from the world as much as she could. She worried a lot about us and strived effectively to provide for us. She always told us, "stay together." I guess that she figured that being together would less the chance of harm, and she enforced these stern instructions daily, weekly, monthly and yearly. I appreciated her welfare for her children. In all the protection that my mother provided for her children against the wiles of the enemy from the outside, she did not anticipate the needed coverage that her girls needed from the inside. Yes, we were covered from head to toe, safe and secured, but she left the back door opened when it came to family. I think it is normal, or it should be, to be able to not worry about the fact that you need to protect your children from family. After all, family is kin, relatives, and your blood.

Psalms 118:8 & 9 warns us precisely, "It is better to trust in the Lord than to put confidence in man. It is better to trust in the Lord than to put confidence in princes." (KJV) The first scripture says, "man" and the second is saying the same thing but instead of stating, "man," he is called by a title, "princes." I'm getting a lot of meat off the bone right now because even though they were specific the first time, they are indirectly saying the same thing twice, which to me is a double warning with the same result. Even if the title is applied, it is still talking about man. Sometimes people hide behind the title, and when the title is not recognized or stripped, you can't find the person.

Anyway, at an early age, the enemy set a trap, the seed was planted, and I was snared. The sad news is that the attack did not come from without but within. Yes, the enemy send the initial attack against my life that left me baffled, bamboozled, discombobulated, and stuck for years. It was sent to permanently paralyze my life. It paralyzed me, but not for life because now I am free. I never found the nerve to tell my mother, or anyone for that matter, because I knew it would hurt her and I didn't want her to feel that way because like I said, she strived hard to protect her girls in the city life.

Born to a set of twins, I always had company. Sometimes the company would be too much company and we would fuss and fight, but we still stuck together. It was in rare form, if you saw one without the other, except in school, but it was a good thing to have someone with you most of the time. As we got older, we started to dislike the idea of having to be with each other, all the time, but we respected my mother's wishes.

Color It Red
Unveiling the Veil

    Growing up in Brooklyn, New York one of the five boroughs called Bedford Stuyvesant, was fun. We lived in a safe neighborhood and during those times everybody looked out for each other kids. The neighbor down the street could "whup" your kids, if they saw them doing wrong, with no explanation needed and send them home. The children in the neighborhood played together outside, but when the street lights came on, it was time to go home. We didn't stay over other people's house but met outside to play together every day. Well having family next door was good and sufficient for all of us. The children still had someone to play with even after the street lights came on, and my mother and aunt would help each other out. Those extremely fun times was when some of the other family members would come visit and everybody would be from house to house. I recall when it was time for those adult talks and they didn't want the children to hear who they were gossiping about; the kids were send to one house while the adults remained next door. Those was some of the most cherished moments of my childhood because I loved times when my aunts, uncles, and cousins came over and family got together.

Of course, our friends didn't like it too much because we didn't have time to play with them because our cousins were there.

Nevertheless, as time went on, one of the family members decided to take advantage of the privilege pass to be inside the family circle. Inside the family circle, there was no reason to guard the children because we were family. Everyone, obviously, did not value the morals of family and out of self-interest one member decided to violate me by choosing to take advantage of that innocent time of my life.

We lived in a building that consists of two families on a floor, which placed the Hope family on the second floor. Whenever company would come over, someone would either throw the key out the window or one of the children would run down and open the door. This is where my twin and I saw no need to be together. One of us could run down, open the door, and no suspected harm to be done, "WRONG!" This is where my predator made his entrance. He was an older cousin, so I guess he should be trusted, so the protective shield was lifted. At first it was cool, I would run down, open the door and we would race back up the stairs which made his visit amusing. Obviously, it was childlike amusing to me, but his definition of amusement formed another way. Then one day, he initiated his hidden scheme. He blocked me from going up the steps and gently slide his hand in my undergarments and while fondling me he put one of his fingers over his mouth and requesting that I make it "our secret." Honestly, at first, I thought it was okay to have a secret and be touched made me feel good because I didn't know better. For some time after that, I was intentionally running to answer the door when I heard who it was because then I would get that "touch" again and it was "our secret." I did not realize how serious this was and that he was trespassing against me and it was not right.

One day during class a group of people came in to talk to us about the signs of rape, child abuse, child neglect, and what to do if you are experiencing them. I remember so clear that one of the signs that it was wrong was when your predator told you "to keep it a secret." I remember it so clear because that's when the light came on in my mind, and I realized that "our secret" was wrong. I was scared and wanted to die, because the group also inform us to tell your teacher, parents, or someone you trust, if this is happening to you. I was devastated because this was family and too scared to tell my mother, let alone anyone else. At this point, I refused to continue to subject myself to these actions. I also began to refuse to go and open the door when I found out who was there. When he got a chance, he asked me, "Why didn't you come and open the door?" I think he caught on to what was happening and didn't come to visit as much. I began to put it all together then realizing from the school teachings that this situation was all wrong; he should not be touching me like this, and there should not be any secrets between him and me. I still could not get up the nerve to tell anyone. Eventually my refusal led me to freedom, but the damage was done. The undeserved, untimely, touch distorted me and dwindled my respect for him. The journey begins.

CHAPTER TWO

Me for Me

Years later during one of my English class assignments, I had to choose a poem, song or writing that was an inspiration to me. I thought it through and chose the famous pioneer and trailblazer, Maya Angelou and her poem, "Still I Rise." Her writings are amazing, and each gives revelation knowledge of real life situations. I am not sure what her intention was when she penned this poem, but while reading it, I felt a connection with her. The situation we shared was similar, but the outcome was different. Nevertheless, she paved the way for me in many areas of my life and I'm grateful. Go to my website, www.dhopechest.com and check out my blog, "Decisions, Decisions, Decisions." There you will find my class paper along with the poem "Still I Rise."

This famous poem, "Still I Rise" intrigued me. My, my, my! It is phenomenal, powerful and prophetic. God empowered that woman with wisdom that could weather any storm and that's exactly what she did. Her silence was weak, but her voice was powerful and prophetic. She rose to be an icon in history and her overall outcome was beyond amazing.

At the age of eight, Maya encountered adversity when her mother's boyfriend contracted his own death papers the day he decided to rape her and was kicked to death by her uncles. Even though this tragedy meant loss of a life, and cost Maya five years of silence, but she exposed her culprit. I believe it was at that point that she realized the power of her words. But unlike Maya, I didn't expose my culprit, didn't know the value of my words, and couldn't rebound from it like she did, but still I rise. Maya didn't play patty cake with the devil. On the other hand, I played Simon Says and struggled, battled, contemplated and bargained with this enemy for years. I gave him the option to choose to free me or keep me bound by remaining silent. I did not know that there was a cost attached to my silence that I would pay for with years of dread. I also didn't know then that I needed to count the cost of this self-torture that was accompanied with guilt from the struggles within.

Maya Angelou's early life experience taught me a few lessons. The first lesson is expose the enemy as soon as you can.

Why be bound when you can be free? Maya freed herself from the yoke that the enemy tried to put on her at an early age by rejecting the offense. She didn't give him the satisfaction of making her a victim. On the other hand, my culprit was free while I was bound. The second lesson I learned was not telling on the culprit freed him but bound me. I was bound by the choice I made not to tell, and it made matters worse. I was trapped in the world all by myself just because I was too afraid to expose that devil. I felt like no one would believe me, help me or rescue me. I tried to save the family's dignity and name while diluting my own self-worth and self-respect. I allowed shame to shut me down. I don't know whether anybody noticed it or not, but I shut down, shut up and became stuck for some time. My situation was not as obvious as Maya's, but I felt the remorse of my violation and the fear to tell. I learned how to muffle the cry within and just be. There were years and years of regret because I could have been free but chose through my silence to be bound.

The third lesson I learned from Maya's decision to expose her culprit is it gave her the opportunity to see revenge on her assailant. I don't believe she intended to see the result to that extent, which was death, but she was free from the worry of tomorrow. She did not have to be concerned about that act ever happening again by that person. As for me, I don't want the end to be that extreme in my case either, just true repentance unto the Lord would suffice.

I, however, submitted to my assailant's action out of ignorance. I assumed the secret was alright for a while, then I recalled thinking about that thing and wondering why he told me to keep it a secret. Then I knew it wasn't ok—neither the act nor the secret. I eventually removed myself from the situation, but the damage was already done, but still I rise.

I was fighting my own battles by myself without the right equipment and protection. Of course, I was losing big time, but who would know? Who could rescue me from me and my inner me? The answer I came up with from a unanimous vote from me, myself and I was nobody, so I continued to battle from within. My enemy was winning without a fight, but my inner me was losing with a fight. Fighting against yourself is a lose/lose situation. You may think or look like you are winning, but in the end, you lose. Oh, my enemy was having a field day in my head, but somebody was praying and covering me. I don't know who but thank you. So here I am in a single parent home, struggling with a secret and not having enough confidence in myself or others to free myself. It looked like the odds were stacking up against me, and they were, so what's next?

CHAPTER THREE

Double Teamed

The struggle to bounce back was too hard for me, so I didn't. I remained numb and stuck for years. I was just existing with a limp. Whether you knew me or not, you would not be able to recognize the limp. I learned how to cope with the limp, but there was no self-esteem, value or endeavors. Enthusiasm to pursue some of my dream jobs like nursing and becoming a teacher was sucked out of me and I was just here. I tried several times to bounce back by joining a dance group, but it didn't help. I attempted to hang with some girls that were rough around the edges that accepted my company and covered me, but the void seemed unavoidable. I even tried to smoke, drink, and party, but that was nasty and scary. I just could not fit in.

To add salt to the open wound, the enemy came again, but from a different angle. If he had come the same way, there was a possibility that I could recognize him and not fall prey. This time the enemy assigned one of his close-knit relatives to trespass against me, and it was a friend of the family. The enemy without was now within. He had gained the trust of a family member and was granted the opportunity to babysit us while we visited their home. My guardian went to the store and we were left unguarded at the hands of an enemy. Your enemy does not care how he gets to you. Just a little crack is all he needs to fulfill his assignment to steal, kill and destroy you. Set for the kill, I was touched inappropriately again. This was added to the limp and I carried on. My enemy was working full time to make sure that he diverted my purpose, but still I rise.

God is so gracious that He covered me through all of this. Even as I write, it is not easy as I relive, release, and uncover this dark side of my life, but God is keeping, covering, and coloring me red! I know that there will be glory after this!

Life goes on and we adapt. By the way, there was never a time when I thought what was happening to me was a part of the norm, but I didn't know what exactly was going on or what to do. Unknowingly, there was spiritual warfare going on in my life at an early age. This was something that I was not used to seeing in my world, and it left a strange feeling on the inside. I didn't question it because I didn't know who to question, but I pondered all this in my mind. All I know now is it was a very segregating experience, and God is the only one who can get the glory for keeping me.

Then the unimaginable happened. The enemy came for me again, but he didn't come alone this time, he sent his sisterly spirit after me. Due to the much too early sexual exposure that I encountered, my mind and body were in combat with the feelings and emotions that resulted, so I was susceptible to more encounters. Growing older and beginning to deal with natural hormonal feelings intensified my battle and I was caught in the crossfire once again. This time it was not someone else, it was with a spirit. Once again, unbeknownst to me, there was a battle going on. At this point in my life, we had the privilege of spending the night over other people's houses besides those in our family. I was at a friend's house, and we did what children do, we played games.

We played church and imitated the adults, we played the board games until someone got mad, lost or cheated, and we played the childhood adolescent game called house. You know the game... it's when you pretend to be a family and act like adults with children and play the roles with responsibilities of adults. There were quite a few children around now, so there were enough to create several play families. There were always more girls than boys and we needed more father figures, so I would play the role of one of the fathers of one of the families. Because I was completely unaware, this was the perfect time for my enemy to resurface and nurture that thing that was now lying dormant within me.

They had kindred spirits and I didn't know then that this was related to the thing that first invaded my life. I still did not agree with these actions, but it appeared that they had more power over me than I had over me. This perverse action began to gain power and I found myself wanting to play house all the time, acting as the father and bumping and grinding. These actions brought back the sensation I received from the previous acts of fondling. I was mesmerized by this feeling and I wanted more and more opportunities to feel this way, so voluntarily or involuntarily, I would impose myself on people until my desire was fulfilled, while selfishly invading and disrespecting others.

This spirit followed me into my young adult life. While trying to get myself together, dedicate my life to the Lord and act like a normal young lady, I encountered more battles of the flesh.

Color It Red
Double Teamed

The devil was working on my demise when I met an older guy that lived in my sister's neighborhood. As I think of it now, seemingly he could see my weaknesses and inner struggles, like I had a bull's eye target on me. At first, he appeared to be that nice, sophisticated, corporate, sexy, good looking, working man, (the smooth operator) but naively, he had gotten involved in a lot of stuff. At first, he kept it hidden well, but eventually it began to leak out and the signs became visible. He attempted to introduce me to his world, but something on the inside would not allow me to agree totally to all of it. Curiosity took over at this time; however, and he introduced sexual intercourse and some of its related activities, like the act of self-gratification, but something on the inside made me very uncomfortable with him and would not allow me to stay in this situation. The Word of God within made me uncomfortable and helped me to gain enough strength to walk away from this situation. He pursued and pursued me, but my heart's desire was to work on pleasing God and I was able to withdraw from the situation. Feeling like damaged goods, but I pursued God. The love, grace and blood of Jesus restored my relationship with God and I felt like I was moving forward, but I was not healed or delivered.

Being insecure about who I was, and my stained past, I began to drift slowly out of the church. I was unfulfilled and confused with all the rules of what I could and couldn't do as a member of the sanctified holiness church, so I began to search for fulfillment elsewhere. Besides the church rules, my mother was dictating what I could and could not do for my career. I wanted to move away for college and she didn't want me to do that. I wanted to go to the army or navy, and she didn't want me to do that. I wanted to become a teacher and she didn't want me to do that. I wanted to become a nurse and she protested that. I obtained a government job in the social security office, and of course, she didn't want me to do that.

To please Mom, I went to the community college but was not happy within so after a year and a half, I quit. Because of who I knew, I had obtained a state position as a Senior Accounting Clerk for the State of New York. Now I was in the position to buy some things that I wanted, including a car, so I did and hit the highway. I started out occasionally traveling to and from Virginia. A portion of my family down there loved to party every weekend, all weekend long and I thought I was strong enough to withstand it, then return to life as usual by Monday. It did not work out that way.

Slowly but surely, I was being sucked into another one of the enemy's traps for my life. Less time for church in New York and more time for traveling and hanging with my partying family in Virginia. Not as strong as I thought I was, but I was able to swing it for a while. In the meantime, I met a nice young man who was involved in church also, but he, like me, struggled with the flesh and we wound up committing fornication. To walk the straight and narrow, we decided to stay apart for a while and determined if it was meant to be, we would reunite. The reunions were booty calls after church, so we resolved that issue by not seeing each other at all. Well the enemy had another plan up his sleeve and this time the encounter wasn't outside the church but inside.

The clergyman that I confided in during my times of struggle now found me to be an open target, even though he was a leader and married with children. This spirit had doom for my destiny, but God had a plan; still I rise. This person had a plan, but

I was naïve to the fact. Occasionally we would run into each other going to and from work, and lunch. Then he started voluntarily waiting for me to get off work and we walked together to the train station. My level of respect for him decreased as he began to express his feelings for me. One day he handed me a small cassette recorder and told me to listen to the message on it.

On one occasion when I arrived at the church, three of the male clergies were standing outside and one of them said, "Sure wish I wasn't married; I would marry you!" and they all laughed and agreed. Distraught by the statement and even the suggestion as being my leaders, I began to withdraw slowly, but surely, from the church. I couldn't hear the Word because of their actions. I attended physically, but my heart and mind were not there, so I began to travel back and forth to Virginia even more.

One Saturday evening the clergyman I mentioned earlier called me and asked me to go with him somewhere for something. I can't remember exactly what he said, but I agreed. Since I wasn't doing anything, I really didn't see any harm in it, and since he was like a father figure in my church life, I didn't anticipate any wrongdoing. Well, he picked me up in a different vehicle than the one he usually drove. It was a van and it did not have any seats in it. I noticed it had a couple of blankets laying in the back on the floor. To make a long story short, this person planned to have sex with me, but I fought and fought and fought and did not give in. I had too much respect for this person and this was crossing the line. He finally gave up and took me home, and since then I could not hear the words that were coming out of his mouth because of the actions I encountered. The next week, he gave me a small cassette player with a message on it. In the message he apologized for his actions, but the damage was done. He went on to tell me how much he loved me and would do anything to make up for what was done. I was done. This was beyond his calling and my expectations of him.

Another clergyman beguiled me, but that didn't last long. He took me to his church and had sex with me before preaching the service. I sat in his office for a while as the service was going on, then came around and sat in the back of the church. Seemingly upset that I didn't follow his instructions to stay in the office, it appeared to me that disguise was all over his face trying to finish his sermon, before taking me back home. All of this stemmed from one wrong touch. By this time, I was feeling like the letter "Q," a big circle with a little tail, and honestly, I did not give up on God's plan for my life. At the time, I was feeling numb. All of this bothered me greatly, but what was I to do? I was barricaded within the thoughts of my mind. Who was I to tell? My mother trusted that we were okay because we were actively involved in the church and didn't run the streets and get in any trouble, but I was dislocated mentally, and I strived on.

I found myself battling with the lust of the flesh spirit, but it did not take away my love for God. I continually found myself at the altar repenting because I wanted to do better but couldn't. It became a stronghold. I was in a cycle bound for hell, but I continued to attend church and meet God at the altar.

To run away from myself and this road of self-destruction, I began taking more and more trips to Virginia for the weekends. Being slowly drawn out of church, I began to encounter the same spirits. One of the mothers of the church politely chastised me with a warning one day after service, but I didn't take heed to it. She said, "You better stop running up and down that highway so much!" Of course, I didn't want to hear what she was talking about, so I kept doing what I was doing. Shortly afterwards I found out that I was pregnant. My mother knew before I could tell her and when I admitted it, she cried, and it hurt me to hurt her.

When I informed leadership of my present condition, immediately I was instructed to write a letter to all the church officers. This was a man-made law because I have not found this action in the Bible yet. An emergency meeting was called before Bible Study and I had to give each officer a letter of my current condition. I was humiliated. The next act completely threw me for a loop. Immediately I was stripped of all my duties. I felt like they barred me from "their" church and cast me aside. Their actions were detrimental; I was devastated, and my spirit was crushed. I could not believe the actions of the "church" folks. Even though I knew I had done wrong and there needed to be some consequences for my actions, where was the love and compassion of Jesus? It was nowhere to be found.

Feeling hopeless and helpless, instead of running back to God, I ran from Him. I packed my car and moved to Virginia. Realizing that it was not the best thing to do, I was hoping to ease the pain that I had inflicted on my mother, church and self and somehow fill the void. Running away from anything is never the solution, but I was trying to close my eyes to reality. Running was a soothing blanket that I thought would eliminate the problem, but it just allowed the problem to lie dormant. The root of the problem remained, waiting for the next opportunity to raise its head.

CHAPTER FOUR
Leaking

Here I am several years later, with three blessed gifts of life called children and leaking. A leak is an unintended hole, or crack that allows a substance to escape, so leaking means a constant flow is being released from you. Leaking does not happen all at once, but it's the slow process of the depletion of all that you are inside. My enemy had me set up, and I could not look up. The sin and shame of my past had me so low that even with the last name Hope, but I still had none. Yes, I was leaking. The poisons of my yesterday and its consequences had me incarcerated with guilt, disgrace, humiliation, issues, insecurity, low self-esteem, no esteem, and no affirmation and it was all leaking into my world.

Searching for love in all the wrong people, just giving myself away, casting my pearls before swine and leaking and losing more and more of me, but the damage was done and now I was living in the consequences of something that was not my fault. I never knew the impact the one action of trespassing against me would have on my life. I just thought it would eventually go away and everything would be alright until the Lord brought it back to my remembrance.

You see, I secretly locked that memory in the subconscious area of my mind by being away from my family, friends, and segregating myself, hoping to live beyond it. I thought I was doing fine, had handled it well and made progress with my life until I tripped over the huge bump in the rug one day. God wanted me to face reality. I ran and hid from it for so long that I had subconsciously convinced myself that everything was okay. You see, you can run but you can't hide, and no matter how long you run, you can't hide from yourself. The voice of your issues may remain silent for a while, but there comes a time when you must remove the rug, stop sweeping around it and expose the dirt. At some point you must face your giant, deal with your past, and confront your pain.

Years and years later, I could still feel the pain of the betrayal. The pain began leaking out in relationships that I thought were going well until some way, somehow, they triggered something that happened in the past and made me think back to my trespasser. It was a *wow* moment for me because I was not thinking about him at all, but suddenly, I wanted to get revenge for what he had done to me. Yes, I was leaking, and my past was surfacing up from out of nowhere. As a matter of fact, it was surfacing up out of the hidden closet in my subconscious. I discovered that for me to move forward and completely remove this out of my heart and mind, I had to continue to let God help me to let it all leak out until it was all depleted and exposed.

I do not write to receive any sympathy or bring hurt to anyone but expose that demonic spirit behind it. If I kept silent, it had the power and authority to continue to run rampant, destroying my life and the lives of countless others. Now that I am speaking up and out, I will defuse its control, break yokes and destroy strongholds with the blood of Jesus. I do not wish my experience on anyone, but I hope and pray that it will become an avenue of healing and deliverance in the lives of others.

CHAPTER FIVE
Broken Wings

Through all of this, I still knew deep inside that I was special, unique and had purpose for living. I was not 100% sure what that purpose was at the time, and sometimes questioned my own self-worth, but deep down inside, I knew that I was chosen by God. Through a powerful confirming preached Word, I concluded that I was picked out to be picked on. Through all my challenges, God gave me Dunamis strength to endure the storms of life. I could not put all the broken pieces together, but I recognized my uniqueness. I tried to run with the crowd and couldn't fit in, and I tried to party, drink, and smoke; that was scary and nasty, and it didn't work for me. All of those were signs of my distinctiveness, but I was still in the making.

One day during a walk through my neighborhood, I saw a bird sitting on the ground. It startled me at first, but as I drew closer, it did not move. It appeared to be helpless. It was still alive but could not function in its capacity. A quick look revealed that its wings were clipped, and he could not do what he should have been able to do. Someone had mangled the bird, stripping it of its privilege. The bird attempted to fly and get away, but was confined, due to the loss of this one capability. He looked helplessly at me. He wasn't confined because of his intellect, surroundings, or circumstances, but his ability to fly had been disabled. Yes, the thing that was necessary and needed for advancement had been detached, causing him to become restricted. I'm pretty sure it was without his consent. Who wants to voluntarily be maimed and cut short of the opportunity to be free to soar high? In the same way, who wants to voluntarily be violated at an early age and suffer the victim mentality for years? Well without your consent, I can answer that question for you, "No One!"

When the Lord gave me this chapter title, I did not know that the term, broken wings, already had a definition. The analogy of the bird gave me confirmation of the title. According to the Urban Dictionary, broken wings refers to someone emotionally scarred, or damaged beyond the point of repair, and it is often used in a derogatory way to describe a girl with a lot of emotional issues. Wow! This was almost a description of me except for one thing: I was not at the point of being beyond repair. Even though I went through what I went through, God had a plan for my life. He didn't leave me irreparable, for he made a way for my escape in due time as declared in 1 Corinthians 10:13.

A bird is an animal that can fly or move through the air with an attached assistant called wings. Even though the bird can soar, a broken wing will prevent it from doing so. The wing enables the bird to be able to do what it can do, and that's fly. When the wing is broken, it lessens the chances of flying, also the competence of the bird is decreased.

When the Urban Dictionary compares broken wings to a state of mind for a girl, I can see the similarity. Because I was at one time in this state, I can say that I was just like a broken winged bird. I had the potential to soar, but I was restricted or confined due to a disability, a broken wing. The wing may or may not have been detached, but it was not capable of operating as it should due to some malfunction. The malfunction was a dysfunction due to a disconjunction: An event that happened earlier in life that brought unhealthy repercussions later in life.

Color It Red
Broken Wings

Broken can indicate a disconnection from your source or lifeline. It can cause dissociation from reality and a lack of coordination. I can also talk on this subject because I too, was separated from reality. I went through the motions and figured my way through, but I was stuck emotionally in a broken wing syndrome. I can clearly recall during elementary school one year when my class was split up into two groups. The first group went to music while the second group participated in another activity. I am not sure what it was at this time, but I remember hating the idea of learning music; even though I love music, but I could not comprehend its language. At the time, due to my issue, I withdrew my interest in it and never returned to it. Now I can see so many buried dreams and desires that remain asphyxiated due to one wrong act. Wow! I never knew the total impact my past had on my future until I began to release it.

CHAPTER SIX
Damaged Goods

Have you ever walked into a grocery store and seen a shopping cart filled with items? The sign on the cart reads, "Damaged goods." Curiosity will cause you to wonder what is in the cart. As you go through the cart, you notice that something is wrong with these items. They are no longer top-quality items. You may see a nick here, a tiny tear there, a small hole here or a dent there. The items no longer qualify to be on the shelves with like products due to some minor mishap. That minor mishap has caused them to be separated. Even though they've had a mishap, someone thinks that they are still usable, fixable, durable and capable of fulfilling their purpose.

Being a part of the damaged goods group, you may find yourself separated, misplaced, isolated and rejected. Due to your imperfections, you are considered as less than, and because yours are showing while others are good at hiding theirs, you are labeled as damaged goods. Damaged goods are still durable, but their value has depreciated. They lack full value due to their mishaps. They encountered some hard times, bumps, and bruises, but through it all, they endured. Damaged goods do not get full credit for being a survivor. Even though they were able to stand the test of time, endure the storms of life, withstand the pain and ridicule, they will be viewed as less than, but damaged goods are survivors.

Second Corinthians 4:8-9 encourages us, "We are hard pressed on every side, but not crushed, perplexed, but not in despair; persecuted, but not abandoned; struck down, but not destroyed" (New International Version). No matter what we go through, it cannot take us down or make us bitter, but it can only make us better and build us up. As a matter of fact, the best witnesses for Jesus are the ones who have been through and have come out on the other side. It is not the ones who scraped their toe and lived to tell about it, but the ones that have been in the pigpen with the pigs and the scraps; survived ridicule; withstood humiliation; endured embarrassment; fought through failures; overcame setbacks and outlived disappointments; these are the ones that God can use.

God can use them because they will all have the same testimony: "If it had not been for the Lord, who was on my side, where would I be!" They will be pointing to the cross as the reason for all their moments of conquering victory. They will be illuminating the blood-stained banner and waving the victory flag. And this is what God is looking for, people who will go through for Christ's sake. They will take up their cross, endure the shame, and allow Him to receive the glory. No, they didn't go it alone or pull themselves up by their own bootstraps, *but God!*

God is getting ready to turn the tables. Damaged goods are also known to be nonperishable. All those who were classified as damaged goods are getting ready to be recycled for Christ. They took a licking but kept on ticking. They have learned to weather the storms of life and continue to live. The nonperishable items can endure and last longer; they don't die or give up under pressure, and they are kept for emergencies. Even though you've had a shelf removal experience and were placed on the dark side of the room because of circumstances, God is getting ready to put you on display. There will be no more backroom exhibits for you. God is getting ready to change your expiration date. Whatever date your enemy gave you and counted you out, God is getting ready to reverse the curse, turn things around and make all things work out for your good and His glory. Romans 8:28 clearly confirms this by declaring, "And we know that all things work together for good to them that love God, to them who are the called according to his purpose."

Damaged goods still can get the job done. Even though their issues can be seen publicly, God is working privately. He's healing them from the inside out and detoxing out everything that is not like Him. Damaged goods hold a greater appreciation for grace. Grace is God's unmerited favor. Even though they messed up and failed, grace grants them another chance to make wrong right. That is why you will find the people of God for whom grace granted another chance, praising and worshipping more, and serving wholeheartedly, as unto the Lord. They appreciate Jesus and His blood that redeemed them from the curse of doom over their lives. If you want to know where the damaged goods are in the church, look for the ones that will shout all by themselves even if the music stops, look for the ones that are worshipping even after the choir has finished singing. If you want to find some damaged goods in the church, look for the ones that wave their empty hands during offering time. They are just so grateful to have a hand to wave to the Lord.

Color It Red
Damaged Goods

Damaged goods are not damaged as we perceive. While people judge you by your income, house, car, job, and bank account, to name a few, God does not judge His children like that. 1 Samuel 16:7 reminds us, "But the Lord said to Samuel, do not look at his appearance or at his physical stature, because I have refused him. For the Lord does not see as man sees, for man looks at the outward appearance, but the Lord looks at the heart." Even though their issues are showing, and their mess is exposed, they hold a special part of God in their hearts. God knew that they would still praise and worship Him despite their damaged goods status, and their praises would be earnestly pure and true.

During those damaged goods times, God is washing, cleansing, and recreating the hearts and minds of His people. You learn how to appreciate things that others take for granted. You draw closer to God and learn how to praise Him no matter what is going on. Knowing that God is with you and for you, helps you to worship and love Him a little bit more. Because we do not praise God only for what He has done, but also for who He is, the praise is real, genuine, and able to flow out, even on a bad day. Damaged goods remember the things that God has done for them and are more than willing to be a living testimony for Him. They are *not* afraid to run and tell that!

I do not believe that God defines damaged goods as we do. While others tend to make being, damaged goods look like a bad thing with inadequacies, through the eyes of God, it is a glorious thing. God knows that He can trust the damaged goods to be trustworthy, dependable, faithful, and more than willing to give all the glory back to Him. If you want to see some damaged goods people, just look around for the faithful servants. Those who are willing to serve in good times and bad, and it doesn't matter what the weather is, they will be there to praise God. God can use the damaged goods because they will be more loyal to Him, willing to bend over backwards and do flips if He asks them to do so. Damaged goods display gratitude in a more profound way. They are naturally sincere about serving. While the Pharisees and Sadducees are working diligently to be seen and heard by man, the damaged goods people are serving, knowing that their reward is in heaven and God will eventually reward them openly.

CHAPTER SEVEN

Spiraling Up

Through it all, I did not give up or lose my faith in God. Even though I was numb to reality and my life was a blur, I still believed that He had me in His hands and everything would be alright. Even though it looked and felt like I was in a no-win situation, my faith kept me holding on. I did not know exactly how, but I still believed. Even when life's experiences and circumstances seemed to be winning, I trusted God enough to stand on His Word. I often reminded Him of His word. One such scripture is, "I will never leave you nor forsake you," and it's mentioned several times in the Bible. Deuteronomy 31:6 and Hebrews 13:5, are reminders to me also. As a matter of fact, I didn't have to look far in the Bible to find a word of strength, encouragement and inspiration in the time of need. God is always saying something that is an on-time word.

As time goes on, you will find yourself in the Word. God will send a preached message that you know was handwritten from the Throne of God, just for you. One message that I don't think I will ever forget was preached by my pastor in 2006, "Come Out of

___

the Closet!" The message was clear to me that not only did God love me, but he had more and better in store for me; but most of all, I did not have to stay where I was, but He was bidding me to come forth. God wanted me to know that I was more than a conqueror and he was going to bring all of what I experienced full circle for my good but for His glory. The process of getting healed, delivered, and set free is not an easy task, but it is possible.

God prepared me for the rough times in my life. This is another example of God's faithfulness to me that I don't think I will ever forget. Just before a life changing storm came in my life, God kept me reading Romans Chapter 8. Every morning when I took the train to work, I would pull out my bible and say, "Lord, what do you want me to read today?" 'Romans 8' was the response. Day after day, month after month, this went on. God was affirming His word within me so that when the winds of life started to blow, this word would be in my mind and spirit, and it was. By then, I had the whole chapter memorized, but continued to read it daily. It was a foundational word for my life, and it had some deep roots that would help me withstand any storm I encountered, and it did.

This was also another instance during which I reminded God of His Word and promises to me. I can testify not from my grandfather's, grandmother's, father's, or mother's lives' testimonies, but I have one for myself. The Word of God is a rock and you can stand on it, lean on it, hide behind it, and if you need to, throw it. It will be what you need it to be: able to grow, maintain, and become fortified for your life's experiences. I have come to learn that the Word of God can do just what it says. God said to Moses in Exodus 3:14, the NIV version, "I AM WHO I AM. This is what you are to say to the Israelites. I AM has sent me to you." God will be whatever you need Him to be when you need Him to be. His Word is sure.

Sure enough, as I continued to attend church, hear the Word, take notes, go home and reaffirm that Word in my spirit by applying and living it again, I was able to start spiraling up. The Word reactivated what was already in me. God pushed the reset button on my life and the Word of God led me forward. It was a process, but God brought me through. Even though I survived and was an overcomer, I was not totally healed nor delivered, yet. That spirit had lain dormant for years, just waiting for the opportunity to raise its ugly little head, and it did. I thought I was over it, done with it and on my way, but because its roots were deep. I was not healed, and it was a stronghold with years of life in me; it returned full force. I thought I was safe, but my enemy had a plan, still working from within.

I met a guy in church and I thought he was all in (church) and he was, but the church was not all in him. We were introduced through mutual acquaintances at the church. I watched him raise his hands and praise God but thought nothing of it at first. Some of my friends and I would meet for breakfast after the first service then return for the second service. This guy and a few of his friends would occasionally meet up with us and enjoy a meal also. After a while, everyone else seemed to have something to do and the circle got smaller until at one point, it was just him and me continuing the breakfast thing every Sunday morning.

We started texting, talking, and enjoying each other's company. He invited my children and me to his house to catch movies, I met some of his friends and my enemy ushered me into the open door. Everything that I was exposed to, running and trying to get delivered from, was reviving itself again. An all-in-one package, so here we go again. At some point, I could literally see the devil when I looked at him. He was a monstrously large creature just laughing and making all kinds of faces. He did scare me, but he didn't bother me because he had me where he wanted me, struggling in a losing battle again.

This time he brought out the same relatives as before and they teamed up. The scripture states in Luke 11:26, "Then it goes and takes seven other spirits more wicked than itself, and they go in and live there. And the final condition of that person is worse than the first" (New International Version). I believe I lived that scripture at this point in my life. I was weighed down and always so tired, extremely fatigued and did not know why. Everything became a struggle: getting up every day and coping, finding a job, working, locating housing, maintaining housing, and being a mother, to name a few.

I struggled and struggled but could not get a break. From evictions, lost jobs, lost vehicles, lost homes, I could not get it together. Not one, two, but three people were depending on me and I could not even depend on myself and get it together. The stronghold was strong and powerful, determined to take me down, but still I rise. I had to go to the doctor every other week to get a B-12 shot; that's how bad I was. My enemy was literally sucking the life out of me. Every time I thought I was able to loosen the grip and start to get it together, that negative force would come again, and I was sucked back into that same cycle again and again.

Let's tiptoe through the tulips because we are not going to give the enemy any more recognition than we must because through it all, he's still a defeated foe because still I rise. I was living on the Eastern Shore at the time and one day, *somebody say, one day!* as I was driving Route 13 in Temperanceville, VA, I heard God loud and clear say, "Whatever you love the most, will rule the most!" It was a "DUH!" "HUH!" and "HMMMMM!" moment in my life. It was an eternal transformational moment in my life, that changed my life forever. I received the key to the door of my deliverance.

God was telling me that I had the power to change what was going on in my world, and whatever I "allowed" to rule me, was what I loved the most. If I loved Him the most, He was the one that I would let rule, but if I loved the things of the flesh the most, then I would let them rule. I immediately began to assure God that I loved Him more than anything and wanted to please Him in every way. It felt like those chains immediately began to loosen off me and I was released from that stronghold; yes, right there in the car.

As I was driving, I began to go into praise and worship and the forces of the enemy began to succumb to the Spirit and I could feel my freedom taking place. Every time God reminded me of those chain-breaking words of deliverance, I reassured Him and myself that my love for Him was more than the love to please my flesh. As I continued to declare those words over my life, the yokes began to be loosed, doors started to open, ways were being made and victory came forth. I refused to allow the lust of the flesh to remain in control of my life. I chose to submit my body, mind and spirit to God's words and ways.

I took charge of my life and the decisions for what my body was going to do and not do. I reclaimed the power and authority that God gave me. He gave me freewill, and I willed to please God. I willed to walk in the statutes of His words. I willed to be pleasing in His sight. I willed to subject my body to the pleasing of the Lord.

The chains were broken, the curse destroyed, and Doris' walk of shame became the walk of tame, and walk of fame.

I gained control over me and was able to tame and bring my body under subjection. I was also able to lift my head up from shame and reclaim my name. Of course, the spectators and investigators of my life noticed my new attitude, altitude, focus, actions, and reactions were different. They noticed because I was ignoring them and their little negative actions and remarks.

I was free and refused to fan the flame that they ignited because God was doing a new thing in me and I was starting to leak again. The leak this time was full of love, joy, peace, strength, and happiness in the Holy Ghost. This leakage didn't flow from the issues of the past, so it was not contaminated, but this new leakage was filled with joy, love, peace, patience, temperance, longsuffering, goodness, self-control, faithfulness, and gentleness. I also had another leakage flowing and that was hope. My hope in God and myself caused the faith in me to regain consciousness and resuscitate Doris. Yes, the Holy Spirit gave me mouth to mouth resuscitation and catapulted me back in place and position in the Kingdom.

I was spiraling upward and enjoying the ride! When you've been down for so long and you become free, you begin to question yourself, "Where do I go from here?" I was so free that I didn't know what to do. I didn't know how to feel, but the feeling I felt was pure, genuine and it felt good. The burdens were off my back, and I now stand confident in who I am in God. Of course, there will still be battles, but I know exactly what weapons to use: prayer and fasting to remain victorious. Of course, my naysayers, haters and imitators wanted to know what was going on in my world. They saw me bouncing back without them. The answer was that I invested in myself. I took another look, and it was from a different point of view—God's!

The Word of God did an oil change, tune up, blood transfusion, and an overhaul all at the same time. I began to think, walk and talk in my purpose. I chose to ignore the "they" crowd because they didn't have a word that would heal and deliver me. They couldn't touch my innermost being and reset me from the inside out, but He touched me! But this time it was not a touch from man! Oh, He touched me! God touched me and made me whole! It was the right touch, at the right time, and it was from the right person—Jesus!

As I began to spiral up, I became empowered by the Word. I felt my strength coming back. I could feel hope coming alive the more I stayed in the Word and was able to learn the Word. In one of the bible study classes at my church, we began to talk about the tongue and how powerful it is. Proverbs 18:21 declares, "Death and life are in the power of the tongue: and they that love it shall eat the fruit thereof." As we discussed the scripture, the teacher asked the question, "How many know the meaning of their name? Some did, but many didn't. As we continued in the lesson, the teacher taught how there is a spirit attached to each name, so when you call the name, you are also calling the spirit assigned to it. So, if you wonder why your child is acting crazy like his daddy, it's because you attached that spirit to him by adding "Jr." to his name!

We laughed and joked a while about it, but we found out that it was so true, and encouraged the young ladies to be mindful of the names they assigned to their children's lives, the negative names we call them, and what we are declaring out of our mouths in times of anger over our children. I pondered on that thing and began to look at some people I knew who had unique names, and some with junior attached to them and my survey proved to be true.

This inspired me to define my name and I made a great discovery. Doris means gift, while my middle name is pronounced Mariah, after the midwife my mother used, but they left off the "h" in the spelling, so I am going to be defined by both. Maria is a very talented person who knows how to make someone smile. She is the person you would want to trust with anything in any area. She is outgoing at times but may also be shy. Maria is the kind of person who will put others before herself. She loves to challenge herself and is very competitive, generous and creative. Mariah means beautiful and perfect. (I'll take that too! Thank you, Daddy!) The name Hope means expectation, anticipation, competent, practical and often obtains great power. People with this name have a deep inner desire to inspire others. So, all this information let me know that I had value, purpose, potential, and promises over my life that I had to fulfill.

I do not desire to leave this world full, but empty, giving out all of me into the lives of others. I realized that I had the ability to become a life changer in the lives of others by being a gift from God to them. All these inspiring words began to feed my inner man as I started to allow these abilities to come alive in my mind as I was unveiled. I began to pursue helping others and continue my writing assignments to empower others. The Word of God informed me in Proverbs 18:16 that my gifts would make room for me and bring me before great men. I've found no greater time to explore that opportunity than now, so I have begun to put it into action.

I was spiraling up because God was pulling me out of that vicious cycle that robbed me for years and caused me to be stuck. I was stuck, but I wasn't slow or stupid. I held on to the Word of God that was full of promises in my heart, knowing that He would do it for me someday and somehow. He did it! God did it! For Me! God cleansed, healed, delivered, saved, and revived me. The song by the Brown Singers reminds us, "If He has to reach way down, Jesus will pick you up!" I was spiraling up and all things were coming together for my good and His glory. Due to total deliverance I was able to maintain in all areas of my life and total victory came to full bloom. (Breathe!)

CHAPTER EIGHT

It's Not Your Fault

Have you ever played the game of monopoly? It's a fun game, but it can consume a lot of your time. This board game can go on for hours, depending on how many players you have and the roll of the dice. As you may or may not know, one roll could land you in jail, free parking, on someone else's property, make you the recipient of rent from guests, you could become the richest landowner, or bankrupt.

No matter how hard you try to strategize, make good decisions and come out on top, the result is not your fault. You can start off good and strong, owning property across the board, but one roll of the dice can change your direction from forward to going three spaces back. You can build houses and hotels on your property, hoping and waiting for one of your opponents to land on them, anticipating a high mortgage payment, only to be skipped over and left abandoned.

It's not your fault that the dice continued to roll from a three to a five, a six to a one, or a two to a four, and that's exactly how life is, full of expectations, anticipations, dispensations, and let downs. The dice represents life and the different things we encounter that monopolize our future. Sometimes it is a high roll and sometimes it's low, but no matter what shows up, just know that it is not your fault. As much as you want to think and believe it, you have no control over what appears on the dice once it is released from your hands.

The concept for the dice is the same concept in life. We can make plans and hope that they turn out as we anticipate, but we never know until the time comes. This concept escorts us into this unpredictable world. While we fight to maintain control over our lives, the things in our lives, including our children, eventually the dice will roll up with a number we were trying to avoid. When that number appears, the cycle of life that holds disappointments, failures, mishaps, frustrations, and aggravations begins to show up.

What are you going to do when things bombard you unexpectedly? Will you tuck tail and run from it like I used to do, or will you buckle down in the ship and endure the storm?

While we try to prevent some things from happening, sometimes it's just inevitable. No matter how hard we work to eliminate mishaps from our lives, they still show up. This is a perfect example to let you know that you don't control *nothing*. No matter how hard you try, it may not work out as you planned. That's another roll of the dice of life, and it's not your fault. It's just the way it is, and there's nothing that you can do about it. Life is strange, and it is unpredictable. Just when you think you have it figured out, the roll of the dice will show you something different. When you need to roll a six, a three will show up; this is when we must learn to deal with what is given to us. The good, bad and ugly all play an important part in our lives.

God reminds us in His word that He has the authority to make all things work out for our good, when we realize that it is all working according to his purpose. (Romans 8:28) This scripture is used often when situations arise, but it is illustrating God's power and not man's. God is sovereign and reigns over the heavens and the earth. The earth is the Lord's and the fullness thereof. (Psalms 24:1) When we move out of God's way and submit to His will, He can do some incredible things in us and through us. The problem is us, and it starts with the man in the mirror. While we can point our fingers and blame others for what's happening to us, there comes a time when we must get in the mirror and point our fingers at ourselves. Even though the dice rolled an unwanted experience for your life, learn to take the time and roll the dice again and again, if you must. You don't have to settle for what life rolls for you, but you can choose to re-roll life.

Some things are not your fault, but most things *are* your fault. It is totally up to you whether you will settle for the roll of the dice. Some things happened beyond your control and you had to suffer the after affects, but there are some things that you had control of and allowed them to become out of control. Even in that situation, you can change the change. Nothing is final and set in stone until you stop turning the stone! You must make up your mind to go after what's good, better, and best for you. You don't have to settle for anything unless you choose to. God operates in an open-door policy. There are no limits to what you can do, be and have, if you take the time to pursue it, and apply yourself. Nothing comes easy. Nothing is free. You must be willing to pay the price with time and energy to achieve more.

Color It Red
It's Not Your Fault

Some unselfish acts were not my fault, but God has taught me to pack my experience under my wings and catapult into my future. Each experience is a lesson learned and a step towards my future if I apply it to my history. Yes, history is a "hi" story that cannot be told better by anyone else but me. It's not my fault and I can't change it, but I can allow it to change me. Yes, my history holds some embarrassing, shameful moments, but whose doesn't?

You can sit and read my story with your five-star nose turned up in the air, but we all have something in our past that we are not proud of. But through it all, my past experiences have made me better, wiser and stronger. They have fortified me to be able to withstand all kinds of obstacles not even related to my experiences, so that I will be able to survive. Yes, I slipped through the cracks a couple of times, but God... God has had a safety net waiting to catch me every time and He has restored me time and time and time again. I am a living, honest testimony that there is nothing too hard for God. He can restore and make you justified by faith. It will be as if it never happened.

Color It Red
It's Not Your Fault

That's where I am now but reliving this experience to write this book was very challenging. I had to remember and feel some of the heartaches, pain, humility, embarrassment, and frustrations that I went through. It wasn't easy, but I know it will be worth it. If I could just help somebody along the way, then my living will not be in vain. If by sharing my life experience, it will help others to share and free themselves, then it will be well worth it. If from my sharing, others will be healed, freed, delivered and restored back to God, then God has accomplished His purpose for inspiring me to write this book. God be praised!

I also believe that God wants me to highlight the fact that it's not my fault. God knew exactly what He needed to be able to expose this spirit and He chose me to endure this, not to degrade me, but empower me to be able to recognize and expose that spirit. Even though it came for me, I fought back. I knew deep within that I did not want to be a part of that kind of company. Through all my struggles, I refused to allow that spirit to possess me. I can recover all, including my children, nieces, cousins, loved ones, and even my enemies. I am fighting back by producing this book.

Color It Red
It's Not Your Fault

CHAPTER Nine

Processed into Position

Life can become a riddle, full of laughter but bearing some heartache and pain at the same time. Through it all, we are reminded once again in Romans 8:28, "And we know that all things work together for good to them that love God, to them who are the called according to his purpose." While so many people throw this scripture around, few truly understand its meaning. When something bad happens and you can't seem to find your way, this scripture is thrown into the conversation. When something good happens and you can see the sun beginning to shine, this same scripture has a way of being worked into the conversation. While God does not renege on His promises, receiving victory and defeat in any area, is a process. To get to the promise, you must be willing to be processed.

Process, according to Google, is a series of actions or steps taken to achieve an end. This means that something desired is not an overnight occurrence but is accomplished through steps; in other words, it will work out if you work it. The steps lead you forward to the desired end, but you must be willing to follow each step. Plenty of times, we want to get to the end of the matter where all the good, better and best resides, and don't want to take the necessary steps to get there. We want to rush through the basic steps that will eventually land us in the place we desire to be, but skipping the process, jumping the line, or ignoring the directions will not get you where you need to be. As a matter of fact, those actions will cause you to miss the mark, and delay the progress. You will be exactly like the Israelites in the wilderness taking what should have been an eleven-day journey that turned into forty years of wandering in the wilderness due to disobedience and trying to do it their way (Joshua 5:6).

There are several things that I want to inform you about the process. The first thing is the process is a process. The process is put in place because there is step–by-step things that you need to do. Second, the process has a specific reason. The reason for the process is because it contains specific directions to help you get where you need to be. You must realize that if God allowed you to face this process, it will benefit you in some way, while giving Him some glory. Everything we face and endure, has a lesson in it. The next thing that you can glean from the process is there will be benefits, but you must follow its instructions. You cannot tell the instructions which ones you are or are not going to do. You must be willing to follow them, step-by-step.

While following the instructions, you must be open to the lesson, is the next thing I want you to know. You must be willing to release your will and way and submit to the steps of the process designed for you. No two walks are alike. God designed each walk according to the person, and each one has a specific lesson attached to it. The lesson is to help you gain some knowledge, wisdom and understanding, then give you the key to the next step. You cannot gain the knowledge, wisdom and understanding doing things your way. You must be willing to submit to another authority to gain something you didn't have from the beginning. Next, I also want you to know that each step of the process is good for you. These steps are designed to help you and not hurt you. Last, but not least, you need to know that the step-by-step process will position you. If you are willing to follow each lesson's directions, the process will cause a change in you. Each step will position you to be in the exact place you need to be. The process will change some things for you, in you and through you, if you are willing to go through the process.

This leads me to think of the life of a caterpillar/butterfly. It is so metaphoric that you may need some understanding to grasp this concept. Even though it starts off being one thing, an egg, the process can transform it into something else, a caterpillar, a chrysalis, and then the beautiful, colorful, unique butterfly. I have never seen two of the same exact butterfly and that's why I mentioned the word, unique, and I believe that is what each one of us is also. No two people are exactly like. Even though I have a twin sister, there are some things different about us. You must read about that in our upcoming book, *The Other Side of Me.*

Now being one thing and becoming another happens through development. You cannot just arrive at a point in your life and then decide that you no longer want to be there. Wait a minute... Oh yes you can, but if you do, you must be willing to do the work and go through the process. The caterpillar is willing to endure the process to become a butterfly. He cannot become something that he is not unless he endures the process. The life of a butterfly occurs in stages and it does not happen all at once. It is a progressive process, but it takes some time. Each stage of the process represents a specific purpose, from forming, developing, and maturing to becoming the product. Each stage must be completed for the finished product to be a success.

There are several other things that the Lord desires for you to know about the process. The process will include the ability to remove one thing and replace it with another. While we are working on becoming a better person, God is removing those things that are not needed nor are they part of your destiny. Even though we encounter so many things along the way in life, some of those things are not welcome in our future. God is preparing you now for later. He does not wait until it is time to receive and enter your next level, but He's starting now on behalf of your later. It is good to know that God knows what you will need later and He's allowing you to receive it, but He does not release it in just any way. You must take some necessary steps to be prepared, in place, positioned, and in the right timing to receive. You can read that in my upcoming book, *If It Wasn't for the Grace, the Grace of God.*

The perfect example of the necessary steps for preparation is a woman in labor preparing to deliver. She must position herself physically in a way for the baby to come forth. Her body must prepare for the timing of the baby's arrival. Everything must work in the correct timing for everything to work out fine. So, it is with what God is trying to do in your life. Like the saying goes, "You can't put the cart before the horse." You cannot do Steps 3,1, and 2, then expect things to go as they should, but if you go in chronological order, the chances are more likely that things will work out as you desire. God set the process in a specific order to work out for your good.

During the process is a time of inventory. This is the time to remove some unnecessary things and people by replacing them with substance that will benefit you. During processing, there must be some reductions. This is the time to do self-evaluations and see things for what they are. This is a time for addition or multiplication, and if need be, division or subtraction. This is the time for applying or rejecting to make up the difference in your life. This part of the process is not up to anyone else but you. You have the power and authority to get rid of anything that is not of value in your life. If that something is not propelling you forward, encouraging you and challenging you to do more and be more, then it is time to deduct it. However, if the thing that is in your life, is strengthening, uplifting, pushing you forward, and allowing you to envision beyond the here and now, then you need to continue to add it to your life. Allow those things to multiply who you are and the purpose for your life. Life is full of potential, but you must be willing to go after it, leaving the deductions and grasping the proliferation of more.

God has endowed each one of us with skills, abilities, and talents that we will never tap into if we don't get positioned for the process. To do and be all that we qualify for, each one of us must submit to the positioning and commit to the process. I just want to encourage and let you know that if God is calling you to it, you can do it. In everything that we must endure, there is something much greater on the other side of it. We must learn to trust God and know that if He tasks you to do it, He will bring you through it. Accept the challenge from God and know that every process is an opportunity to put you in position for greater, better and best.

The scripture in Hebrews 12:6-11 also educates us: "Who the Lord loves he chastens and scourges every son whom He receives. If you endure chastening, God deals with you as with sons, for what son is there whom a father does not chasten? But if you are without chastening, of which all have become partakers, then you are illegitimate and not sons. Furthermore, we have had human fathers who corrected us, and we paid them respect. Shall we not much more readily be in subjection to the Father of spirits and live? For they indeed for a few days chastened us as seemed best to them, but He for our profit, that we may be partakers of His holiness. Now no chastening seems to be joyful for the present, but painful; nevertheless, afterward it yields the peaceable fruit of righteousness to those who have been trained by it."

Color It Red
Processed into Position

Whew! If we would learn to take a licking and keep on ticking, then we would have the ability to become partners with Christ in His sufferings and in His holiness. The reward is greater than we could ever imagine because it is not only temporal, but it is eternal. While many strive to be pleasing and acceptable according to their outward appearances and accolades, God is interested in the heart of the matter. Where do you stand and what is being processed through the issues of your heart? God is working to process you through His filtered word. God's word is not discriminatory for just the elite, but it is neutral, and everyone can grasp its concept. God is willing to patiently wait while we process ourselves from ourselves. It is not until you are willing to let go of your will and accept God's that the possessing into position begins.

CHAPTER Ten

It's Lonely at The Top

One day while interacting with one of the sisters after church service, out of nowhere she said, "It's lonely at the top!" I paused because her statement caught me off guard, but it was so true. Those words hit my spirit and remained in my mind. The next time I had a chance to talk to her again, I reminded her of our last conversation, hoping that she would elaborate on it, and she did. Briefly she talked about how she had worked hard to accomplish some goals in her life and how people had acted and treated her while she was trying to better herself. I found what she was saying to be true in every area of my life too. She went on to say, "The higher you go, the thinner the air." Another thought to ponder, but I could identify with what she was saying.

The statement, "It is lonely at the top," truly hit home for me. While we are souled out for God, determined to please Him, and while courageously exposing the enemy, there will be times when it is going to be lonely at the top. Sometimes it feels like the weight of the world is on top of your shoulders, and your enemy has his foot on your neck. Even while you are working on coloring it red in your life, your enemy will be working on coloring you dead! Yes, wants you to "Poof, be gone." We all have an enemy assigned to us and his job is to steal, kill and destroy (John 10:10). We are not trying to highlight him and his works, but just expose his tactics. While you are doing the best, you can with what you've got, he will send all kinds of ideas, thoughts and discouragement to make you think and look like you are fighting a losing battle. He wants you to think you are in this all by yourself and you will never be able to conquer the things that are trying to conquer you.

As a matter of fact, he whispers in your ear the same thing that this chapter is named, "It's lonely at the top!" He attempts to put ideas in my head like, "You are trying to expose me, but nobody is going to believe you and you will be left standing alone. You are trying to empower people with your testimony, but you don't even know if anybody is going to read or believe what you are writing!" Nevertheless, I am going to continue to work on this project just to let my enemy know that it does not matter what he says or does and his suggestions of what the result might be don't affect me. God told me to write it and I am determined to do so. To my readers, I'm writing to let you know that it is going to be a lonely walk up the path of righteousness and exposure. Everyone is not willing to go with you nor will some want to hear what you have to say, but you must be willing to walk alone. The lonely road is challenging but necessary. If you are willing to strive upward, there will be some unavoidable bumps in the road. You must continue to go on despite the barriers.

The place of transparency is going to be a lonely place, but you must also be willing to get naked, tell the truth, and let the pieces fall where they may. I want you to know that some will not like it and question why you are putting your business out there like that. Well my answer to that statement is if you've been through what I've been through, you would run and tell it too. God brought me through, healed, and delivered me, I have no choice but to tell it. Even when others may try to make me feel ashamed and embarrassed for what I endured, I can say, through it all, I made it! God afforded His grace, mercy, and unconditional love in

_____

my life so that I can gratefully tell others what He did for me. My experiences can become someone else's life lesson. Even though I endured it, they don't have to, but can trust God to do for them what He did for me. No matter what you must face, God will bring you through to the other side with victory.

One of my mottos is, the best person for me to be with is me! I've learned how to enjoy being by myself, and I love it. I love hanging out, eating, and sometimes enjoying a movie by myself. It's not until you can enjoy you, that you will be a pleasure and blessing to others.

No matter how lonely it gets in your walk of life, dare to walk alone. It is a good place to be because you know that you are not truly alone. God is with you and for you. Allow Him to encourage and strengthen you as you walk by faith and not by sight (2 Corinthians 5:7). Sometimes you must walk alone because of the assignment on your life. You cannot take everyone with you and everybody is not going to be for you and what you stand for. You can rest assured that there will be opposition, but stand on God's word, and do what He told you to do. It will be lonely at the top, but I'd rather be lonely and obedient than to be in the crowd and disobedient. God will recompense you for your faithfulness to the work of the Kingdom.

Lonely at the top can also be an indication of your feelings while you are releasing and freeing yourself. It doesn't necessarily have to mean that you are above everyone else, but you can feel the weight of your past being released and you are being uplifted from the sinking sand of your past. Yes, the thoughts, ideas, encounters, and circumstances of yesterday have a way of making you feel like you have a millstone around your neck and you are at the bottom of the sea. The enemy doesn't want you to expose him or become free from the pain of yesterday, so he sends a spirit of discouragement, depression, oppression, and embarrassment so that you can quit in the middle. There are many of you even now who have had the ideas, thoughts and desires to write and expose the enemy of your life, but the drive, enthusiasm, and courage is not there because you are worried about what people are going to say or think about you afterwards. That was the same challenge that hindered me from stepping out before now, but my love for

God in my life outweighs the opinions of people. I am at a point right now where I do not care anymore what people say or do to try to discourage me. I know what God told me to do and if I do what He says, He will take care of the rest.

I'm thankful that I serve a God who is concerned about my whole being. The things that concern me, He is concerned about it also. There is nothing that comes my way that He is not aware of and He promises to take care of me in all areas of my life. What matters the most in my life right now is that my God is pleased, and if He is pleased, I am pleased, and everything else will work out.

Sometimes you must encourage yourself. There will be times when you are your only encouragement. While we can be our own worst critic, we can also become our best cheerleader. Take the time to believe in yourself and the things that God is doing in you and through you. Dare to trust that God is working on your behalf and time will tell the rest of the story. As you stand on the Word of God and do what He told you to do, you must pause, pat yourself on the shoulder, and keep working. I must warn you in advance, do not expect encouragement from anyone.

When people find out that you are working on an assignment for the Kingdom, there will be plenty of distractions. Plenty of invitations will come your way to attend different functions, go out to eat, shop, and engage in different activities, but you must be like Nehemiah, who was focused while he functioned in his purpose. He heard the words of discouragement, threats, and invitations, but he did not allow them to deter his purpose. He continued because he had a mind to work, and work on his mind. I encourage you to read the book of Nehemiah; it is a perfect example of being productive even with opposition.

Please know that you will never be alone. Even if the feeling of being lonely attempts to invade your mind, remember that God is true to His word that assures you, "He will never leave you nor forsake you" (Hebrews 13:5). Don't allow the word lonely to be a part of your vocabulary. Allow the Word of God to conquer every spirit of discouragement that comes to stop and block your progress. They are assigned to abort your purpose, but persevere through it all, and let lonely be left for those who don't have a destiny to pursue or a vision to obtain. Keep it moving!

CHAPTER Eleven

The Canvas of Life

In this chapter, I am going to tread lightly because this subject is also a topic in the sequel, "Color It Red! The Power of Forgiveness." The canvas of life is full of lines. There are a few lines that are straight, but there are many that are crooked, wavy, long and short, vertical, and horizontal. Some of the lines have knots in them from the twists and turns of life, but each line represents something.

While we try to manage each line to perfection, there is a tendency to cross your line. It can become entangled with another line and lose itself. It can also encounter another line and begin to soar above its present state. Each line's objective is hidden within itself.

A canvas according to Wikipedia is an extremely "durable" plain-woven fabric used for making sails, tents, marquees, backpacks and other items for which sturdiness is required. This means that a canvas can endure some stuff. There was nothing outstanding or magnificent about the canvas, but it did its job. It carried a heavy load and functioned under pressure. A canvas can take a licking and keep on ticking.

A canvas sounds just like the lives of many of us today. Many of us can say that we've endured some stuff. We were able to endure because we had the right equipment to carry the load, and function under life's pressures. God empowered us with a canvas. We were fortified with a durable sturdiness, as required. He gave each of us what we needed to be able to triumph through our trials. Since we will not all encounter the same mountains, God distributed to each according to their ability or need. He equipped us with the right sources for the right forces. We have what we need to deal with what we are up against.

The canvas of life was designed by our creator, God. Even though there are no two identical canvases, each one can do what it needs to do to display His majestic splendor. Each line, however long, short, crooked or wide it is, will represent an event in your life. The line does not stop short, but it can connect to another one and sometimes it stops and sometimes it keeps on going.

Color It Red
The Canvas of Life

God created the canvas so that you can have a visual of who you are and what you have endured. While we give God the glory for taking us through life's situations, He wants you to see and know exactly how you made it through. Someone once said, "Life is a canvas of many strokes where shades from different palettes meet into a picture so concrete that some forget it is their own." The many strokes indicate that you didn't give up or give in to the pressures of life. Sometimes it was so confusing and mixed with a variety of colors at the same time on the palette, but the result still displayed your unique inner beauty.

A quick look at your canvas and you will be amazed at how much you've endured and how one line or situation connected to another caused you to be able to continue. When we take the time to ponder all the things we've faced, endured and triumphed over, it will amaze even you. God wants you to view your canvas and see how far you've come and what you've accomplished in your life. Sometimes we don't acknowledge our own endeavors because we can't comprehend how far we've come. Even though the process is long and hard, you are making progress. Being able to view your canvas of life and see for yourself where you are, will enable you to release the vitality to continue, knowing that you are developing day by day, event by event, and line by line.

Let the canvas of life take you for a ride back down memory lane for a moment. Remember some of the hardships you faced and didn't know if you were going to make it, but you did? How about the times when the bills were due, but you didn't have the payment? Some way and somehow, you made it. How about the need to provide for your family and there were no extra funds to do so, but some way and somehow, it worked out. Yes, you gave God praise and appreciated how He made a way out of no way. God wants you to know that He made a way because you made the way for Him to work on your behalf.

Your trust and faith in Him caused Him to be able to move on your behalf and make the impossible possible. Yes, your leaning and depending on God colored your canvas with lines that express success stories. It's not just because of God's hand of provision, but your willingness to be put in that place of exposure that produced for your good but for His glory. So, scan the canvas of life and take the time to appreciate your growth.

CHAPTER Twelve

I Believe I Can Fly

The different colors of a butterfly are so captivating that sometimes I just sit and watch the butterfly fly until I can't see it anymore. Each color stands out and collates with the others to display the butterfly's uniqueness. I wonder if each color could represent the struggles that the butterfly endured, what would be said. What if each color had a specific meaning and defined a specific characteristic or a solemn defeat in the life of its owner. While there are so many different beautiful colors, each with a different meaning, I only want to talk about red right now, but I encourage you to explore the meanings of other colors.

According to Google, red is the color of fire and blood, so it is associated with energy, war, danger, strength, power, courage, determination as well as joy, passion, desire, sensitivity and love. It has a very high visibility. Red is also a very emotionally intense color. It enhances human metabolism, increases the respiration rate and raises the blood pressure. Since colors represent something, I'm wondering what the colors of my uniqueness as a butterfly would be. Since I've endured some stuff, and there are some things that no one will ever know, what if it could be displayed through my colored life as a butterfly.

From a caterpillar to a butterfly, each butterfly can fly above their past situations as a caterpillar and be free. While some endured the process to become a butterfly, they are soon cut off. Swatted by a newspaper, smashed by a car tire, or eliminated by the wind, and they don't have the opportunity to live beyond their success. Something occurred that cut their lives short. But there are some of us that endured to endure. Even the trials of life cannot shortchange us of our future and purpose. We survived intentionally to become victorious instead of a victim.

While we were enduring some things, the colors of life were beginning to form within us. I feel like my butterfly would display a little bit of all the shades of colors. Life has not been easy, but now I can see why it was well worth it. If I didn't have a problem, I would never know God could solve them. The glory of the Lord shall be revealed through my life. I believe I was created

_____

to be a world changer and make a difference in someone's life. The struggles of life and its victory have possessed me with the ability to fly.

"I believe I can fly!"

There's a song called, "I Believe I Can Fly" and it's been sung by both Glee Cast and R. Kelly. As I compared lyrics, I found something meaningful in each of the versions, so I have decided to elaborate on the ones that connect with this chapter. Let's chat about the Glee Cast version first. I love the way it starts out with a positive, confident statement. He started out with winning in mind. With faith in yourself, there is nothing that you cannot do. With a positive attitude and the right perspective, I believe I can fly. There are times when it seems like you can't hear anything that is encouraging you to go on, not even from a song or the voice of God. Everything is silent, and the silence is loud. Even in times like that, you must learn to keep the faith. I love this verse that declares I can't be defined. Now they are talking about me!

While so many people think they know me, very few are telling the truth. While people try to define me by my circumstances and situations, they really don't know me because those temporal things can never declare who I am! I have come to realize that while people attempt to put a label on me in accordance with their little mindset, they will never be able to understand who I am and what I am unless they search for me according to the Spirit. I laugh at them and "SMH" because I cannot be defined by the natural eye because I am a spiritual being. You must be in tune with the Father to know me. Neither my possessions, my status, nor anything else can define me. God defines me! And He does not reveal Himself or me to everyone. As a matter of fact, the circle is very small of the ones who really know me. I love the fact that many think they know me, but in some ways, I'm still a mystery to them. Hmmmmm! Now that will preach, and the sermon topic will be, "Don't judge the book by its cover!"

Just because my struggles, and battles are out in the open, it doesn't mean that God is not with me. As a matter of fact, the struggles prove that He is with me because I keep bouncing back! Now that will preach also, and the sermon topic will be, "I got a bounce back anointing!" Alright now! Nevertheless, I am not a girl that can ever be defined! The last interesting verse I would like to share from Glee Cast goes something like, when you endure, the no becomes a yes. And that's exactly what life is all about: striving through opposition and not allowing anyone or anything to dictate what you can do. The sky is not the limit, you are! You are your own success story. Write your own ending, then work hard to attain it. Don't accept no for an answer, but let it encourage you to strive, and dig a little deeper while you overcome all hurdles of negativity.

Now R. Kelly's version had a few different verses that I would like to connect to this chapter also. Did you know that he sang this song during his audition on The Voice where he held the note for 8 minutes and 91 seconds, and the anointing fell on the audience through his endurance?

The end of the first verse declares I can do it if I can see and believe it! Well this is a powerful statement because it's talking about faith in yourself. After you've trusted in others and perhaps they failed you, the trust in yourself will keep you afloat and moving forward. Seeing yourself doing what you dream of doing and believing that it is possible, is over half the battle. Now it's time to put feet to your faith and do something. The lyrics said that "I," which means that each person must take personal responsibility for their own faith and what they see and believe. Each one of us can only see from our own perspective. No one else can view your perspective about you but you, and their opinions don't count.

The next verse says that when you have faith to believe in yourself, it will give you the ability to fly. It is just a matter of taking the limits off yourself and God. He can do anything, if we can just believe. The following verse contains powerful words that focus on the fact that my ability to achieve begins with me. I am convinced in my heart that there is nothing impossible for the ones who can see themselves achieving before they achieve. One of Vicki Winans' songs proclaim that to have what you want, you first have to see it, and it is so true. Life is full of miracles for those who can just believe, and it starts on the inside.

Then the R. Kelly version of "I Believe I Can Fly" goes on to encourage you to believe you can climb to limitless heights. I am also highly influenced by my faith that you don't have to be a bird to soar, just be a determined individual with the right perspective and attitude. Your attitude determines your altitude. A positive attitude will take you further than a negative one. Spreading and stretching your faith will allow you to increase and overcome any obstacle.

Both versions of the song make the same statement about being able to touch the sky. Now this declaration is full of faith. Even though the sky is miles away, faith will persuade you to believe that there is nothing impossible for you, nothing you cannot do, if you believe in yourself.

I conclude this chapter with these thoughts: Even though life experiences professed that my life was a broken wing due to circumstances, God has given me the ability to prophecy over my life and declare, I believe I can fly, and like a wounded soldier, I am not going down without a fight! I am determined to recover. I may not attain all that I could have, but from this day forth, I put a demand on my stuff and call it from the north, south, east, and west and decree that I shall spread my wings, stretch my faith and soar into my future with purpose. There is nothing that I cannot do if I put my mind to it. I pray that God will red flag all opposition from this point on and cause them to fall by the wayside. Lord, help me to recognize all distractions, defuse them at once and not allow them the opportunity to take up residence in my heart and mind, as I focus forward.

"Lord, I believe I can fly. I believe that I can soar above all the negative events that have bombarded my life to try to take me down. I believe that I have the Dunamis power to get the job done and complete my assignment. I know that you have equipped me with everything that I need to be effective for the Kingdom. Help me to regroup as you reset my life and repair every area of brokenness. As I allow forgiveness to remove the pain, I pray that your Holy Spirit will soothe the sting and rejuvenate my inner being with fresh oil that will flow like no other. In Jesus name I pray. Amen!"

CHAPTER Thirteen

Pre-Approved for Greatness

In 1977 there was an R&B singing team, McFadden & Whitehead who came out with a famous hit that rocked the charts in first place for weeks called, "Ain't No Stopping Us Now!" I remember being in the park with my older sister and everybody that had a boom box had it turned to the popular station, WBLS, and a certain time every day they would play this song, and everyone was jamming at the same time. If your boom box was not on the station when the song came on, you didn't have to worry because everybody else around you were tuned in. The words of this song gave us a sense of unity, strength, courage and the hope to keep on moving. Now the long version played for over ten minutes and everybody knew the words to the song and it was like one big family affair. This song was an encouragement to everybody to hang on and press forward. I took the words literally. Today, I still remember the lyrics, but what I loved the most was when the verse kept repeating the words, "No Stopping! and in one of the verses it proclaims we're leaving negative people way behind!

The vibe I got from this song is a good segue into the meat of this chapter. Now you may wonder how in the world I got that topic out of that song, but if you keep reading you will connect. While there were many obstacles, traps, and snares thrown in my way to dissuade me from getting to this point in my life, believe it or not, when those hard times came, this song came to mind, along with many others that helped me to make it through. At some point in my life, I had to be self-promoting to persevere. I could not allow those stumbling blocks to fog my view, so I learned how to turn them into stepping stones and keep it moving. "No Stopping!" was imparted in my mind for tough times like this. I've learned through the words of this song that there will be difficulties and challenges along life's road, but quitting was not an option. I could not stop and detour from my purpose, no matter how hard the battle got. I'm still here today because I heard the words from this song ringing in my head. I wish I could write out the whole song for you, but you should check it out. No, it's not a "church" song but it's a positive, inspirational song that outweighs some of the songs sung in today's churches.

Pre-approved is an evaluation of a potential borrower by a lender that determines whether the borrower qualifies for a loan from the lender or determines the maximum amount the lender would be willing to lend. However, God does not operate through that system. According to the protocol of the Kingdom, you don't have to be a potential borrower depending on a lender to determine whether they are willing to assist you because God has already taken care of all the necessary paperwork, approval package, co-signer, and put a down payment on the cross. God sent His son, Jesus to qualify you to be pre-approved for the things of the Kingdom. All you need to access your pre-approval award is the faith to believe and receive because it's already done. In God's pre-approval program, you are not only approved for a car, house, lawn mower or motorcycle. His benefits include eternal life, favor, blessings, hope, joy, peace, love and victory, to name a few, but it will also   be well worth applying for His life insurance policy.

_____

As we grasp the fact that we have been qualified for pre-approval from God, it's time to add the security of greatness also. We don't have to work to earn it, because it's a given by the Father. Ephesians 3:20-21 proclaims, "Now to Him who is able to do exceedingly abundantly above all that we ask or think, according to the power that works in us, to Him be glory in the church by Christ Jesus to all generations, forever and ever. Amen" (New King James Version). God desires to bless His children. It is an honor and privilege for Him to give to His children.

God not only set you up for a pre-approval of all that He has for you, but He wants it to be exceptionally distinguished. Psalms 27:5b states, "He shall set me up upon a rock." God is ready to put His people on display and let the world see what He is doing for His children. Even though there is so much chaos going on in the world, it does not stop the hand of God from moving on behalf of His children. What God is getting ready to do for His children will be mind-boggling and nobody will be able to take the credit. I truly believe that God is up to something and those of us who are in position and prepared will be able to receive it. He is going to do it in front of all your haters, naysayers, doubters, and commentators. Those who counted you out, did not have faith or trust in you, and pushed you to the side like a reject, will be left overwhelmingly amazed with their mouths open in awe.

And when He does it for His people, He is going to put you in a place or position that others will be able to see it. The Word says He will set you up upon a rock. A rock is high and is visual to all. You will have the anointing of the disparate person that God created you to be. Your past will have nothing on you and all the lights of God will be so bright that some folks from your past will not be able to recognize you because of the glory.

We are talking about the pre-approval of greatness that is upon your life. First Peter 5:10 boosts us on by proclaiming, "And after you have suffered a little while, the God of all grace who has called you to his eternal glory in Christ, will himself restore, confirm, strengthen, and establish you." You are going to be recompensed for all that you've been through. God said, Double for your trouble and with interest! I believe and receive that Word for myself! Hold my mule while I praise Him right now! I had to share that Word with my Facebook Family! I'm not sorry, but I truly believe that God is up to something. All the signs are there. There is so much opposition against the children of God, but it is only pushing us into position. Just like birthing a baby, the contractions are putting the baby in position to come forth. Whew! I feel that thing!

First Corinthians 2:9 reminds us, But as it is written: "Eye hath not seen, nor ear heard, nor have entered into the heart of man, the things which God hath prepared for those who love Him" (NKJV) The children of God do not even know what to expect from Him. All I know is it is going to be greater and better. Haggai 2:9 confirms this fact by declaring, "The glory of this latter house shall be greater than of the former, saith the LORD of hosts: and in this place, will I give peace, saith the LORD of hosts. I am not sorry. I believe God's Word!

The J.J. Hairston and Youthful Praise singers sing a song titled, "After this." This very encouraging song reminds us that it does not matter what you are facing right now, it will end, and God will get the glory after all of this! And it will be the pre-approved

greatness of God.

Esther was preapproved for greatness, but she had to go

through the purification process. And so, it is with each one of us;

we must be willing to do what we must do to be placed in

position for greatness.

CHAPTER Fourteen

I Serve the God of the Impossible

Healing, deliverance, and victory over any situation is not impossible for the God of the possible. It may seem like it's an impossible task, but the God I serve is the God of the Impossible. Impossible to you, but possible to Him. I am a living witness with a testimony that the Word is true in 2 Kings 3:18 declaring, "This is but a slight thing in the sight of the Lord: He will also give the Moabites into your hand." God is going to take care of the things concerning you and give you the power of your enemies in your hand! Powerful because that thing or person that thinks they have the upper hand over you, will fall prey to your hand. It is amazing how God turns things around for us. Those things that appear to be on us, will be the same things that we will be able to use to step up and over our obstacles. God is turning stumbling blocks into stepping stones.

While others doubt my success and celebrate my downfalls, I come to serve notice on my enemy. Through it all, I serve the God of the Impossible. What appears to be impossible to you, will be the exact thing that God will use to show your doubters to be liars like their father.

My situation, circumstance, even my future appeared to be dark, blurred, and close to hopeless, but the God of the Impossible showed up and made all things new. It looked impossible, but His appearance is always on time. He knows what to do and when, so that it is right on time.

I just want to encourage you to hang on in there. We do not face the same trials but know that the God of the Impossible can make it possible. There is nothing too hard for Him. Put your trust and hope in Him, He will not let you down. You can't look at the situation and compare it to the ability of God, nor can you look at your situation and compare it to others. You must believe that no problem is bigger than God, and God is mightier than my problem. We must learn to take the focus off the situation and turn it on the Almighty God.

Luke 1:37 reminds us, "For with God nothing shall be impossible." Do you want to know why this declaration is being made? Well I'm super excited to be the one to tell you. Impossible is stating that there is no way for it to be. God is the God of the Impossible because God is saying, "Impossible is possible because I'm possible!" Impossible is saying that God is the only one who can do it. He is the only one who can make the possible out of the impossible. God is the only one with the ability to make it work. No one else can make this statement, "I'm possible," but God. We are all limited but He is unlimited. "I'm possible!" is God's decree to all our need. While the dying world is attempting to make it without God, that is an impossible situation, God has put a plan in place in which He can prove His "I'm possible" abilities, but we must be willing to accept His help His way. This is where the problem lies. We want God's help, but we want it our way. We want God's results, but we want them our way, and of course, it doesn't work like that. The God of the Impossible can make it possible, but on His terms, and not ours.

I am constantly continuing to work on removing myself from the driver seat and allowing the Lord to have His way. This is a constant battle because we think we know what's good for us, but God knows what's best. Join me in asking Jesus to take the wheel and allowing God's will be done.

The God of the Impossible has made it possible because He is the "I'm possible!" Matthew 11:29-30 reminds us of the God of the Impossible capabilities by declaring, "Take my yoke upon you and learn from me, for I am meek and lowly in heart: and ye shall find rest unto your souls. For my yoke is easy and my burden is light."

Can God? God Can!

CHAPTER Fifteen

It's Time to Color It Red

My sister and my brother, I am telling you the truth; it is time to color it red. It is time to do something about your past and your future. The past has held you captive with memories, thoughts and feelings for years, while your future, at the same time, is constantly beckoning you to come forth. You've been at a crossroad for years; now is the time for you to decide, and it only takes one. How long are you going to stay where you are, betwixt and between your yesterday and your tomorrow? How long will you be willing to stay in the emotions of the past? Are you ever going to recalibrate the whole situation and change the direction of your wind? The wind is always blowing. The wind that is blowing in your life can blow north to south or south to north, parenthetically. It is going to blow, but you have the control of which way it is going to blow. Is it going to blow from good to good, good too bad, bad too bad, or bad to good? This is your life, so this is your call.

Things happen, but like the scripture says in Psalms 107:2, "Let the redeemed of the Lord say so, whom He has redeemed from the hand of the enemy." It's time to say, *"So!"* It is time to say something to your past. It is time to say, *"So!"* It's time to talk back to the thing that keeps talking to you. When it says, "It happened." You need to say, *"So!"* When it says, "You failed!" You need to say, *"So!"* When it says, "You lost! You need to say, *"So!"* When it says, "You messed up! You need to say, *"So!"* and on and on and on. Let the redeemed of the Lord say so! It does not matter what happened in the past; you can recover. God is not ignorant of your life experiences, but He doesn't want you to be ignorant of the fact that they are not the end of the story. God is trying to rewrite the script with you in it, but you can't move forward looking backwards. History is good knowledge, but the future still needs to be written.

It's time to become your own success story. It is time to make the ripples turn into waves. It is time to become your own rainbow. You don't have to display all the colors of God's rainbow, because that's God's. Learn how to create your own rainbow and glow from its reflection.

While the rainbow represents the reminder of the covenant that God made with the earth in Genesis 9:13, coincidentally, in the making of the rainbow, He started with the color red. This has a very significant meaning to me because it is highlighting the main point of this book. (Hang in there and you will be blessed.) Red has the longest wavelength in the rainbow, with each color decreasing from that point. This sounds like red is the most needed color. (Pardon me for a moment, but this chapter is starting to sound like a prophetic declaration to me, and I praise Him in advance.)

The representative of red in this book is the blood of Jesus. In the making of the rainbow, God started with Himself. He started with something that would stretch beyond the now and move into years to come. And God took the red, the blood and covered the rest of the colors. God used His blood to cover His children, the world and the earth. The point I am trying to make right now is if you start out creating your rainbow with red, God and the blood, the sequence of all the other colors does not matter; whichever order they are in, they will be covered. So, it is with the rhythms of defeat from the past, it doesn't matter what happened to you in the past, you are covered by the blood. It is time to start extending the most significant color of the rainbow across yours. It is about time to start painting a different picture, singing a different song and dancing to a different beat.

It is time to color your past, memories and wounds, all the same color—red. The past should no longer have a say in your life unless you allow it. It is time to do something about your past and it is time to do something about your future, at the same time. It is time to dip your brush in the only color that matters right now. It's about time for you to get the paintbrush of life, approach your canvas with confidence, and begin to glide the red paint across everything that held you captive, stuck and unproductive in life, and eliminate the past. Allow the blood of Jesus to wash and cover your agony of yesterday, while you pardon the pain and dismiss the damage. All the frail pieces from those situations that seem to lie in your path of progression, are a part of your past that you need to let pass. Pass over them. Let it go and let it be. Free them so that you can be free. Discharge them so that they don't destroy you. Defuse them before they demolish you.

Earnest Pugh wrote a song titled, "God Wants to Heal You." The purpose of this book, *Color it Red,* is to let you know that God wants to do a new thing for you, but first He must heal you. You are like a broken-winged bird, leaking, and double teamed by your enemy, but God wants to heal you. He wants to restore you and make you whole and complete. It's a process and God is willing to walk out the process with you if you are willing to allow Him to lead the way. I am a living testimony that God can heal you everywhere you hurt. Healing, deliverance, and total victory is a process and I'm still in it, but it sure feels good where I am now compared to where I was at the beginning. I thank and praise God that He loved me enough to want healing and wholeness for me and was willing to be patient with me while I kicked, hollered, screamed, and fought against His will and His way. But praise be unto God, there will be glory after this.

CHAPTER Sixteen

The Rainbow

Vickie Winans wrote a song called, "The Rainbow," and it talks about a storm that won't seem to pass.

When this song first came out, I drove an hour to a bookstore in another state to get the CD. At the time, I had to have it. I wanted to hear this song repeatedly, mainly because it was singing my tune. I was in a storm, but I was looking for my rainbow. I was determined to get this song. As I recall, I was prepared to drive another hour to the flea market in yet another state to locate this song. God was ministering to me through the words of this song, and it became my rainbow as it gave me strength to endure, hope, and persevere.

If you'd been through all that I'd been through, you would have gone that extra mile also to hear a word of hope. This is what this song did for me at the time. Even though I was in a storm, deep within I knew that it wouldn't be like this always, but I needed a little push to the next phase. I needed help, knew I needed help, and was willing to go after it. This point makes me say, "If you know you need something, how bad do you want it and what are you willing to do to get it?" I worked hard to position myself in the right place to get what I needed from God. I knew He was the only one who could help me.

The rainbow reminds us of the covenant that God made with Noah and the Earth of how He would not destroy the Earth by water, but by fire next time (2 Peter 3:5-7). There is also another symbolic meaning from the rainbow. The rainbow also represents hope. As the rainbow stretches across the earth, it extends a piece of hope. When you see the rainbow, there should be an expectation beyond what you see, and a belief for more. Even though the rain has stopped, and the sun is peeping through the clouds, there are a lot of people who still cannot grab onto hope for a better tomorrow. Their expectations are shot with no zeal to look beyond their current situation. If you observe them carefully, you will see them join in and rejoice at the celebration, but shortly thereafter, the smile is gone, and the look of despair quickly recaptures their demeanor. Their days are dark and gloomy with no desire to anticipate more. While others may do their best to give words of aspiration, deep down inside there is no fire, hope, or zeal.

For people without the right introspective, a positive projection, and a poor retrospective, hope tends to be catapulted into the zone of despair without much assistance. They can't seem to see the forest for the trees. There is no hope or anticipation of a rainbow. After enduring so much, some refuse to continue to look or believe again. They feel like theirs is a hopeless case. Life circumstances have suppressed any opportunity to dream again, so their vision is blurred, and they feel stuck between a rock and a hard place.

I'm writing to challenge you to look, dream and believe again. As a child of the Most High God, I want to let you know that there is still hope for you. I'm declaring rainbows in the sky. There is a rainbow on the other side of what you are going through. In 1 Kings 18:44 the prophet was praying for rain, so he sent his servant to go and see if he could see the cloud coming. The servant did not see it, so the prophet sent him back again and again, but the seventh time he went to look, he came back with a different report. It reads, "And it came to pass at the seventh time, that he said, Behold, there ariseth a little cloud out of the sea, like a man's hand." This is encouraging us to continue to look and believe, knowing that something is going to happen for us. It may not happen the first or second time, but you must be persistent in your faith declaring, "I don't know when and I don't know how, but I know it will happen for me!" This is the mindset that I had. I kept coming to church and believing God. I kept the Word in my heart and pondered on His promises.

There is a special designed rainbow with your name on it. God has orchestrated a unique symbol of His love for you in the form of a rainbow. The colors of your rainbow are carefully picked by Him. Each color incorporated is selected to represent your life experiences. While the colors of God's rainbow include red, blue, orange, green, yellow, indigo and violet, you may have different colors to define who you are, but the selection is not up to you. God chose the colors of your rainbow to remind you of what He brought you through.

Color It Red
The Rainbow

The rainbow is representing the covenant that God continues to have with you. God's Word is true when He proclaims in Hebrews 13:5, "I'll never leave you." You endured and survived because He was with you to walk you through. Even though there were some lonely and tearful nights, God was right there, and He continues to be there. Therefore, you can't throw in the towel and give up the fight. There is a rainbow that you must create. You create your rainbow by living beyond what you endured. The scars of your past create a color in your rainbow. The failures of yesterday create a color in your rainbow. The wrong decisions and mishaps you encountered all create a color in your rainbow.

When you get to life beyond these things, you qualify to add another color to the rainbow. God allowed you to come through on the other side so that He could make your rainbow colorful. If we never had a problem, how would we know that God is a problem solver? If we'd never been sick and needed healing, how would we ever know that God is a healer? God is something else and proclaimed it so in Exodus 3:14 when He declared to Moses, "I AM THAT I AM!" This is some serious stuff because if you have the one who can be everything you need Him to be, when you need Him to be, then you don't have anything to worry about because you will make it through.

The rainbow is also there to remind you that there is still hope for you. Take the time and examine the beautiful colors that God picked out for your rainbow. Allow each color to define itself to you. You know what you've been through and endured, so choose to celebrate it with the colors handpicked by God. Allow your rainbow to extend you from the past into your future. Accept the past, no matter what it contains, for it escorted you into your present. You would not be where you are now if the things that happened to you did not happen. It does not matter whether they were good or bad, they had the ability to position you to your now. Look and you can see that you are not where you used to be and it's because of the things of your past. They assisted you in deciding to do something different to cause a change. The things you endured were a stepping stone to your present and if you allow them, they can become another stepping stone into your future.

Color It Red
The Rainbow

The rainbow is full of hope. It consists of the ability to keep believing. The rainbow ignites your inner man to live on. While circumstances attempt to kill him, the inner man continues to fight now. We all have that inner ability to fight, but we must be willing to do so. While the fight is in us, it must also become a part of us. We must allow it to do what it do and that is to continue to wage war against all opposition. If we silence our inner man, then who's going to lead the fight? Our enemy is not going to encourage you to fight for what is right and rightfully yours.

The rainbow sparks the hope within. The different bright colors empower you with strength to keep the faith. God never promises you a life without trials and trouble, He gives each of us the ability to be able to handle them. The rainbow gives us the visual of hope. It captivates the energy of the earth and distributes it with glamour with color.

God wants you to know there is nothing you went through that He cannot use for your future. The good, bad and ugly, God has the power to use it all for your good. Even though there are some things that we are not proud of and if we had the choice, we would choose to keep them hidden in a closet somewhere, but God is saying, "I want you to use that; yes, those embarrassing, and humiliating events that brought you shame and blame." These are the tools God is willing to work with to bring Himself some glory. God said, "I don't need those stories where you crossed every "t" and dotted every "i." I can't get glory out of that because it is all a lie and a fake. What I want to expose are those things that occurred when circumstances pushed you into horrifying moments, when you couldn't help yourself and I was able to get my glory because you knew it was nobody but me who brought you out!"

God is not interested in exhibiting artificial believers who act like they've never been through anything and if they have, they tell the story like it was their own ability that delivered them. They already have their glory, but what God is interested in exposing in this day and age are the ones who have been through hell and some hard places and realize that if it had not been for the love, grace, and mercy of God, they know they would not have survived. These are the qualified candidates for God's next move on the earth. The ones who were healed from diseases, delivered from drugs, and set free from bondage and now they are souled out for the gospel of Jesus Christ. The candidates must be willing to become naked and not ashamed of the testimony of Jesus Christ. They are willing to run and tell that!

The rainbow has one more purpose: it is designed to escort you from your past into your future. It wants you to know that your future is so much brighter than your past. If you look at a rainbow, you will see only bright, vibrant colors. In the rainbow there is no sign of dark or cloudy days, which is an indication that the worst is behind you and the best is before you. The rainbow expresses life, uplifting help with joy, peace, and hope. It can get you from your yesterday, today, and into your tomorrow. If you check out the rainbow, it is stretched from one place to another. It is extended over space. We have no precise indication of how far the rainbow spreads, but we know that there is a mighty distance from its beginning to the end, so it is aligned with your past and your future. They are so far apart that you will not be able to see one from the point of view of the other. You must start moving from one towards the other. Allow the rainbow to lead you from your past to your promise, and from your failures to your future. Yes, there is a rainbow in the sky for you!

CHAPTER Seventeen

Conclusion

"This is the divine hour and set time, saith the Lord, for my people to come forth and pull the covers off their enemies. I have given my children the power and authority to do so, but many refuses to walk in my strength. Time is up for the enemy and the hidden schemes that he hides behind in the world and in the church. I am turning the tables, pulling off the covers and exposing every demonic spirit in the Body of Christ. I refuse to allow my genuine children to become tainted by the deceptive mannerisms that are operating in My name. These operations are pulling the wool over the eyes of My children and trying to deceive My elect called-out ones. The world is confused because it is said to be done in My name, but I do not have a part in it. There will be much exposure in the days to come. I refuse to allow My name to be polluted by the schemes of the world. Many will see and recognize the difference."

I just want to encourage you to take the time to color it red. Take the time to evaluate your life and the things that are not beneficial for your present and future—color it red. Let the past pass. It is time to leave the past where it belongs and that's behind you. God knows everything about you. He knows your past, present and future. He made a way that your past does not have to cause you to forfeit your future, and that's through Jesus Christ.

Jesus came to offer Himself for all our sins and connect us back in right relationship with God through His blood. Allow the blood of Jesus to do what it was created to do, and that's to wash away everything and everyone that is not a part of your future. Your future is so much brighter than your past, and it holds nothing but good for you. Your future is like the rainbow that God displays periodically that is full of hope.

We must be willing to use our God-given power and apply the blood. *Color it Red* is encouraging you to use the gift God gave you to make your life better. Nothing and no one can cause you to abort your future unless you allow it. *Color it Red* is doing something about your present and future by erasing your past. We are not promoting forgetting the past because you need the memory to help you to see how far God has brought you and to know that you are not exempt from trouble.

We, however, want to help you to release the things that mean you no good and will not in any way help you to move forward. These are the things that need to be colored red by the blood of Jesus. There are some things that cannot go with you into the future because they do not belong.

You've learned the lesson and now it's time to move on without them. Color it red and continue. Color it red and move forward. Color it Red and become the beautiful glistening butterfly that God intended for you to be! COLOR IT RED!

www.ingramcontent.com/pod-product-compliance
Lightning Source LLC
Chambersburg PA
CBHW060312050426
42448CB00009B/1797